"HELP, HELP, GET US OUT OF HERE! I CAN'T SEE! I CAN'T MOVE!" they cried. Without hesitation, Basil climbed on top of the table, and there in the darkness he held the tent up over his head with his strong arms. Animals of all kinds and sizes scrambled out from under the tent into the pouring rain. Basil's arms ached from holding up the heavy canvas tent, but he managed to hold it up until everyone had escaped.

"Thank goodness Basil was here!" someone yelled as the animals ran into the forest for shelter.

Life in the ghetto

ghetto

written and illustrated by

ANIKA D. THOMAS

LANDMARK EDITIONS, INC.
P.O. Box 4469 • 1402 Kansas Avenue • Kansas City, Missouri 64127
(816) 241-4919

Dedicated to
my mother Barbara
who encouraged me and believed in me;
and a special thank you
to my dear departed sister Shono
who inspired me and will always be
a major factor in my achievements.
Without them in my life,
I could not have written this book.

COPYRIGHT © 1991 BY ANIKA D. THOMAS

International Standard Book Number: 0-933849-34-6 (LIB.BDG.)

Library of Congress Cataloging-in-Publication Data
Thomas, Anika D. (Anika Dawn), 1976-
   Life in the ghetto / written and illustrated by Anika D. Thomas.
   p.   cm.
   Summary: A thirteen-year-old black girl from Pittsburgh describes what it is like
to grow up in a tough inner-city neighborhood.
   ISBN 0-933849-34-6 (lib. bdg.)
   1. Thomas, Anika D. (Anika Dawn), 1976 — Juvenile literature.
   2. Afro-American children — Pennsylvania — Pittsburgh — Biography
      — Juvenile literature.
   3. Inner-cities — Pennsylvania — Pittsburgh — Juvenile literature.
   4. Pittsburgh (Pa.) — Social conditions — Juvenile literature.
   5. Pittsburgh (Pa.) — Biography — Juvenile literature.
   [1. Thomas, Anika D. (Anika Dawn), 1976-
   2. Afro-Americans — Biography.   3. Inner cities.
   4. Pittsburgh (Pa.) — Social conditions.
   5. Children's writings.   6. Children's art.]

   I. Title.
   F159.P653T468   1991
   974.8'860049607302 — dc20
   [B]   91-13944
                                                          CIP
                                                          AC

Editorial Coordinator: Nancy R. Thatch
Creative Coordinator: David Melton

Printed in the United States of America

Landmark Editions, Inc.
P.O. Box 4469
1402 Kansas Avenue
Kansas City, Missouri 64127
(816) 241-4919

LIFE IN THE GHETTO

When Landmark initiated THE NATIONAL WRITTEN & ILLUSTRATED BY . . . AWARDS CONTEST FOR STUDENTS, we never intended that all books in the series of *Books For Students By Students* would be pretty picture-story books. From the beginning, our goal has been to publish a strong cross section of ideas, projecting the wide spectrum of experiences and interests of students.

While we love books that entertain, we feel it is important that we have the vision and the daring to also select books that offer insights into human conditions.

When I read Anika Thomas's LIFE IN THE GHETTO the first time, I was so struck by the emotional impact of the narrative, I immediately turned back to the beginning and read the story again.

When copies of the book were sent to our national panel of judges, I hoped they, too, would be receptive to such a bold departure from the other students' books we had published. I was not to be disappointed. The majority of judges agreed and determined LIFE IN THE GHETTO to be the First Place Winner of the 10 to 13 Age Category.

In her extraordinary book, Anika does not present a pretty picture of her childhood experiences. As her narrative unfolds, the vivid scenes she describes become etched in the reader's mind. And her impressionistic line drawings add insight into how she sees her environment, her family and friends, and the threats which surround her.

Anika has written about her life with conviction and candor. One cannot help but be touched by the courage of this young girl to tell of the problems she has faced and to offer her hopes and dreams for us to share.

— David Melton
Creative Coordinator
Landmark Editions, Inc.

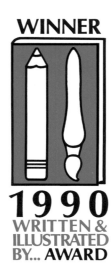

WINNER

1990
WRITTEN &
ILLUSTRATED
BY... AWARD

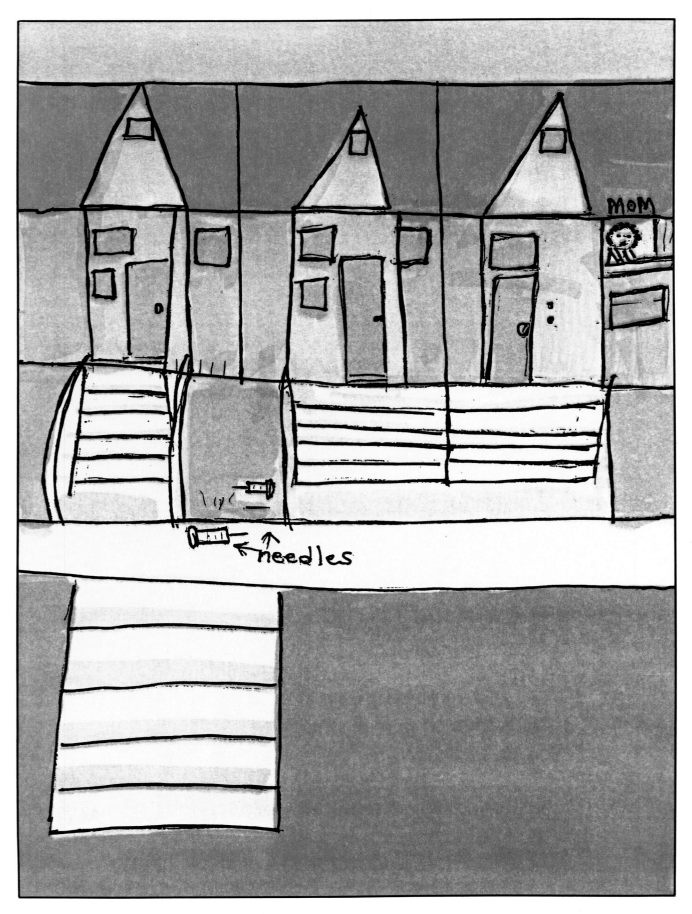

Mom, Daryl, Darcy and me. We care about each other and try to be happy in spite of everything.

We moved to the uptown district of Pittsburgh, Pennsylvania, when I was sixteen months old. I am thirteen years old now—old enough to take a good look at this neighborhood and know that it is not for me. In fact, no decent person should have to live here. I hate this place!

My mother and I live on the second floor of an apartment building. My niece and nephew, Darcy and Daryl, live with us. They are twins. They are nine years old. When our car was working, my mother would take us different places, just to get us away from this neighborhood. But since the car broke down, we are stuck here most of the time.

Once in a while, the twins and I get to jump rope or play hopscotch on the sidewalk in front of our building. But we never are allowed to go outside unless my mother can watch us from the window.

I used to wonder why my mother wouldn't let us go out and play like the other kids do. Now that I am older, I can see for myself. I understand what my mother means when she says, "There's too much mess going on out there."

There are drunks on the sidewalks and in the streets all the time.

One of the eleven women who live in the downstairs apartment.

No Respect for Anyone!

Our area of Fifth Avenue is run-down and dangerous. So many of the vacant houses on our block are boarded up. That makes the neighborhood look even worse. There are a lot of bars on our street, too, and drunks are all over the place. Drug peddlers and addicts are everywhere. No matter the hour or day, there is always something disgraceful going on.

Eleven women live in the apartment below ours. They go in and out, slamming doors at all hours of the day and night. They don't wear much in the way of clothes. And they stand on the steps in front of our building, waving at men and flagging down cars. Men go in and out of the women's apartment all the time.

These women have no respect for us kids or the older people who live here. They don't get along with each other either. They're always yelling and getting into fights. We hear them argue a lot about drug money. I often see drug needles lying around outside our building.

Next door to us is an empty house. The people got put out because they were selling drugs. Then one of them broke in and stole some of the water pipes. Several houses on our block, including ours, had no water for nearly two days. A couple of doors over, there is another empty house. Those people got kicked out for selling drugs too.

Last week there were two fires set in another "dope house" three doors down from us. After the first fire, the landlord told the people to move. A day later the second fire was started. Everyone suspected the tenants had set the fire, just to get even. My mother and I are afraid someone will set a fire someday that will burn us all up.

There are hundreds of dangers in our neighborhood.

No One Seems To Care

The kids in the house on the corner are always in trouble. By the time they're fifteen or sixteen years old, they've become parents. There's always a new baby girl or boy in the house. But none of the teenagers act like parents to their babies. They leave that up to their grandmother who lives there. And she's drunk more than she's sober, so she doesn't know what's going on most of the time. I've seen some of her younger grandchildren smoking and drinking beer in the empty lot behind our house. They're just little kids who are between four and eight years old.

One girl who lives at that corner house is named Kim. She is sixteen years old. Kim is the only decent person in her whole family. She smiles and talks to me. She is always nice and never too busy

Troublemakers

Kim is a real friend.

to help me with anything. She taught me how to roller skate and jump rope. Whenever she's around, she won't let her cousins hit me. I really like Kim.

Most of the children around here stay outside as late as they want. Sometimes they are out until three o'clock in the morning, and they are very noisy. Their parents aren't home much. And if they are, they're usually drunk.

In fact, almost all of the people in the neighborhood drink a lot. Since my mother doesn't drink anything stronger than Pepsi Cola, she keeps her distance from everyone. She says she has little in common to talk to these people about.

My Mom Minds Her Own Business

My mother doesn't go out much, except to church or to the clinic for medical treatment. She prefers to stay to herself. She says most people around here want to know other people's business, but they really don't care if you live or die. So she just smiles at them and says, "Hello" or "How are you today?" I am very happy to have a mother who stays at home and takes good care of things.

The twins and I have to go to bed at eight o'clock every school night. On weekends, as long as we don't make too much noise, we can stay up until we get sleepy. But school day or not, we get up between six and six-thirty in the morning. Mom can't stand to sleep late. When she's up, she wants everybody up.

There used to be a nice lady who lived on the first floor of our building. Her name was Mrs. Bell. She was really friendly and always said, "Hello" and "How are you?" I wish more people around here were like her. Not long ago Mrs. Bell moved away. Good for her! But we sure miss her.

Much of the time, I feel very sad inside because we have to live here. In this place, every day seems the same as the day before and each night is like the one before it. Every night I pray that someday we can move from here. I call this place *The Ghetto*. It is all I am used to, but I see it for what it is. I want out!

I wish more people were as nice as Mrs. Bell.

I Don't Know Why They Act That Way

I remember the first time my mother allowed me to sit on the front steps by myself. Four kids who lived down the street came up and started calling me *white honky* because my skin color is lighter than theirs. They said a lot of swear words too. Then they kicked and hit me. I started crying and went into the house.

Another time my mother and I were outside. When she had to go in to answer the phone, the four kids came after me again. They called me more names and hit and kicked me. They stuck up their middle fingers at me. I had never seen anyone do that before. I didn't know what it meant, so I stuck my finger up at them.

Then I heard my mother call out the window, "You'd better not hit my daughter again!"

The kids ran home. But a few minutes later, they came back with their older sister. My mother was waiting for them.

The older girl said, "I want you to know — your child stuck her finger up at these kids!"

My mother replied, "My daughter doesn't know what that means, and neither do I. So you and those kids had better get out of here and leave us alone! And don't any of you ever kick or hit my daughter again!"

After they went home, my mother said to me, "Now do you see why I don't let you go outside alone?"

Those kids still haven't changed. They love to cause trouble and get into fights. Mom doesn't like to argue and fight, but she isn't afraid of those children or their older sister. When I'm outside, my mother won't let those kids come near our house. She watches over me like a hawk.

There's Always Something Going On!

I look out our front window a lot. Believe me, there's always something to see. Police drive around in patrol cars and watch our neighborhood day and night. Sirens wail at all hours, and we often hear gun shots after dark.

Sometimes the police help us. But other times they beat up on people for no reason at all. The other day I saw a man and woman arguing as they walked down the sidewalk. A police car came by and stopped. Two policemen got out. One of them grabbed the man and threw him against the car. After they handcuffed him, they started banging his head against the hood.

While this was going on, the woman kept screaming, "Why are you hitting him? He's my husband! He wasn't doing anything!"

Then a police van pulled up and two lady cops got out. After they talked to the woman a few minutes, the lady cops suddenly grabbed her and pushed her into the van. The policemen shoved the man inside the car. Then all of them drove away.

I would like to go away too—away from the terrifying noises and awful scenes. Everywhere I turn I see ugliness.

Rats, Roaches and Mice!

The rats don't come inside our house, but they tear into the garbage cans outside. I've often seen dogs eating live rats. A couple of months ago, I was sitting on my porch and saw this happen right in front of me. It was disgusting!

I have seen roaches — hundreds of them — inside our house. We call the exterminators to come and get rid of them. The exterminators spray in the corners and behind the cupboards. Then we don't see any roaches for awhile. But nothing helps for long. After a few weeks, the bugs are back.

I really hate it when the roaches are high up on the ceiling and we can't get to them to kill them. It takes a long time for them to come down, and sometimes we take a long time watching them. As soon as a roach finally comes down, we squash it with a newspaper.

I've heard that the women downstairs leave garbage and filth all over their apartment. My mother says this is the reason we have so many roaches and mice in the building.

We use mouse traps, poison, and even "mice glue" to kill the mice. If only a mouse's tail gets caught in a trap, my mother takes a shoe and kills the mouse. That may be a terrible thought, but having mice running around in your house isn't so nice either.

I hope I'll win a sweepstakes someday. If I do, I'll move my family out of here first thing!

Some days I was afraid to go to school.

Kids Can Really Be Mean!

I don't know why the other kids don't like me or why they want to pick on me. Maybe my light skin is the reason. Or maybe it's because I'm not as street-smart as they are.

It bothers me a lot when kids call me names and hit me. I hate them for it, but I just don't say much about it. I try to mind my own business and be polite to everyone. It's the way I was brought up.

My mom has always told me: "You go to school to learn, not to get into trouble." Most of the other kids don't seem to know this.

When I was a first grader at A. Leo Weil School, I was treated very badly. Some of the kids in my homeroom cursed me, hit me, and pushed me down when the teacher wasn't looking. On the playground, they got their friends to join in. At first I didn't tell my teacher or my mother.

One day a girl in my class asked to see my ten-karat gold ring. When I held it out for her to have a look, the girl grabbed my hand and took the ring. I didn't tell my teacher, but that night I told my mother. She called the principal, and he promised to get the ring back. But he never did.

The second grade was bad too. A girl took my watch off my desk. I told my mom when I got home, and she called my teacher. The next morning my teacher asked the girl if she had taken the watch. The girl said "No, I did not!" But I was lucky this time. The girl was wearing the same dress she had worn the day before. When the teacher checked the girl's pocket, there was my watch.

The third grade was even worse. Some kids threatened me and hit me so much, I was scared to go to school. One day my mother gave me money for school pictures. After I paid for them, I put the one-dollar bill I had left over in my desk. That afternoon a girl took the money. It made me really mad! My mom was upset, too, and she called my teacher. But we never got the money back.

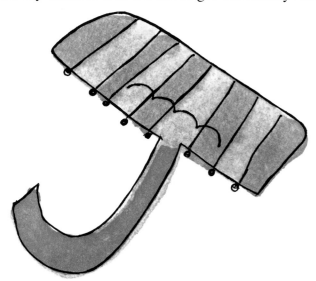

When I was a fourth grader, someone took my new umbrella out of my locker. My mother called the principal and told him she wasn't putting up with the stealing anymore.

When the principal talked to the girls in my class, they began accusing each other of having taken the umbrella. One of them even said she had seen who took my dollar the year before. But it ended up with the principal not doing anything else about the umbrella or the money.

Then there was the problem about my eyeglasses. In the fifth grade, a boy pushed me down the steps and my glasses were broken. Now my mother was really angry because eyeglasses are expensive. She called the principal, but he wouldn't give her the boy's phone number or address. He said he would try to reach the boy's mother and ask her to phone my mom or meet us at school to discuss the matter. But the boy's mother never called us, and she never showed up at school either.

When I was in the sixth grade at Prospect Middle School, an older boy stopped directly in front of me and spit in my face. I don't know why he did that. But nothing was ever done about it because I had never seen the boy before, and I didn't know how to find out who he was.

Having Big Brothers Can Be a Definite Plus!

That same year an eighth-grade boy kept pushing me around on the school bus and putting salt in my hair. He was sixteen years old and a lot bigger than I was. When my mother found out about it, she told my brothers.

Well, my brothers, who are both over twenty-one, went to see the boy's father. The man promised his son would not bother me again.

But a couple of days later, the boy hit me. That really made my brother Bob angry. He took me by the hand and led me down to the store where the boy's father worked. The man was there and so was his son because the boy worked at the store after school. My brother was ready to beat up both of them.

When the boy's father saw my brother, he knew his son had been bad again. He grabbed his son, knocked him down several times, and made him promise he would leave me alone. The boy has never bothered me since then.

Things Are Looking Up!

I'm now a seventh grader at Prospect Middle School, and there is a new principal who handles things a lot better. His name is Mr. Pipkin. He's very friendly and knows most of the kids by their first names. He is also fair and takes care of problems quickly.

For instance, in class one day, a boy walked over to me and touched me on my breast. When I told my mother what had happened, she was furious!

That evening she tried to find the boy's home. But after a while, she got tired of knocking on doors and asking where he lived.

The next morning she went to the school. I've never seen my mother so angry. She walked into that school like she was going to destroy it and said loudly and clearly what she had to say.

Mr. Pipkin promised he would take care of the matter, and he did. He also told me if anyone ever bothered me again to come and tell him immediately.

My mother had advice for me too. She told me she and my brothers could not settle all of my problems for me. She said I needed to learn to stand up for myself.

Not long after that, a girl beat me up after school. My mother was really angry. But when I asked her to go to school with me and settle the matter, she refused to do it.

"Not this time, Anika," she told me. "You're going to have to take care of that girl yourself. When you get to school tomorrow,

I like Mr. Pipkin. I think he is the best principal in all of Pennsylvania.

you better have *fighting* on your mind. You fight that girl again, and this time, you had better win! If you don't, when you get home, I'm going to give you the worst spanking you've ever had!"

I knew I had to do it.

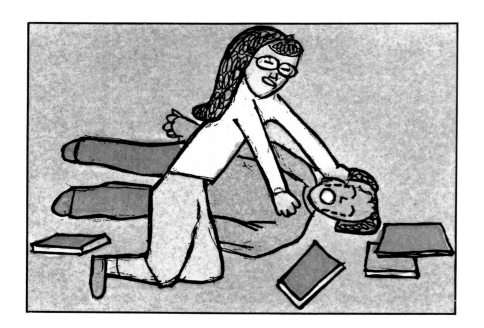

When I came home the next day, I was smiling. I had finally fought back and won!

Surprise!

Yesterday was report card day. My niece and I make the honor roll every report period. But this time I was surprised! For the very first time in my life, I made the HIGH HONOR ROLL! Mr. Pipkin bought me a sundae to celebrate.

I called my best friend, Alishia Washington, to tell her about it. She's thirteen years old, too, and we've known each other since we were in the second grade. Alishia now goes to another school, so we don't get to see each other very often. But every day we talk and laugh for hours on the telephone. Alishia and I want to go to college together. We have so many hopes and dreams.

I'm going to start taking ice skating lessons soon. I know I'll like that. I sure wish I could see Debi Thomas skate at one of our local rinks. I am crazy about her. She's my idol and my inspiration for wanting to become an ice skater.

I would like to become a singer, too, or maybe an actress, and I think it would be exciting to work for a newspaper. My mother tells me I can be anything I want to be. She says, "Go for it, Anika, and don't let anyone turn you around."

I am sure going to try.

I want to be an achiever. Mom says I can be anything I want to be.

Not As Much As Some—But More Than Others

Today it is so hot, and I am so sad because we live here. I wish I could go outside where it's cooler, but I can't because my mother is still at the welfare office. When she gets home, I know she will be in a bad mood. She's always in a bad mood after she's been there.

Every six months my mother has to go to the welfare office and fill out government forms. If she doesn't, we won't continue to get welfare. The worst thing is that she has to go so far to get there. And when she finally gets to the place, she has to sit there and wait for hours to deal with questions that only take a few minutes to answer.

I don't blame my mother because we can't afford to move out of our neighborhood. Her welfare check only comes to $316.00 a month. My mother hates being on welfare, but her health is poor and she's not able to work full time.

When I'm feeling sad about living here, my mother tells me: "We may not have as much as some people, but we have more than a lot of people." She reminds me that there are people who don't have a roof over their heads or enough food to eat. My mother seems to always know the right words to make me feel better.

I know we are luckier than many. My mother manages her money well. We wear nice clothes, and we have good shoes on our feet and warm coats for winter.

And there's a warehouse right behind our building that supplies the food banks. The man in charge is named David. He's a real friend to the twins and me. He gives us candy and cookies, and a couple of times he called us over for a cookout on his lunch break. David also gives my mother all kinds of food to help us out. He understands our hardships. I love him like a brother.

My own brothers, and my sisters, too, help us by buying things we need. Our family is very loving, and we look out for each other.

Sometimes one of my brothers gets us tickets to concerts or ice shows. In the summer months, my sister spends a lot of time taking us to parks. My brother Sandy has a very nice house with a big yard. The grass is a pretty color of green with no bare spots at all, and it's tabletop smooth. We love to visit his home!

Feelings of Joy

My family belongs to the St. Benedict the Moor Catholic Church. I love that church! Every time I enter it, I get a warm feeling. The people who go there are so nice. I especially like Father Vallone. He makes everyone laugh, and he's always so kind to children. I wish all the kids who live around here could go to that

Mom is really a good cook and the best mother anyone could have.

Me at my First Communion.

church, or one like it. I think it would improve their attitudes and their behavior too.

At church I sing in the children's choir. I really love to sing in the Christmas plays and the masses. Our choir goes caroling at senior citizens homes during the holidays too. And we visit shut-ins and sing for these lonely people. It makes me feel good to make other people happy.

Father Vallone is kind to everyone, and he makes us laugh a lot.

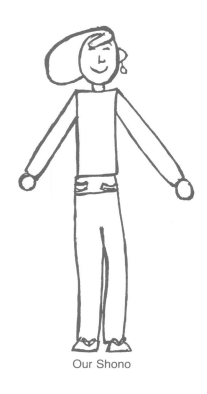

Our Shono

They All Leave Home

I'm the youngest of ten children. I have five brothers and four sisters. The boys are the oldest, so they left home before any of my sisters did.

When we first moved here, my sisters still lived with Mom and me. Then they grew up and left home. I was afraid my mother might go away too. I used to worry a lot about that. I remember crying and begging Mom not to leave me.

About a week after my first two sisters went to college, my third sister got married and left us too. Suddenly everything seemed different. One week I had four sisters in the house; the next week I had only one sister still at home. Her name was Shono.

All my sisters used to give me baths, play games with me, and take me places. Now I was very lonely. So I started clinging to Shono. We only had each other, I felt. I thought Shono would always be with Mom and me. But when Shono was twenty-eight years old, she left us too. On July 20, 1988, she died.

You see, Shono had epilepsy. Without warning, she could go into a seizure at any time and fall down. One day she fell down the steps at a neighbor's house. When some kids laughed and made fun of her, Shono started crying and ran home.

"They're only kids," Mom tried to tell her. "Don't pay any attention to them."

But Shono couldn't stop crying. She went upstairs and packed a suitcase. I was up there and asked her why she was leaving.

"I'm going away because I hate this place!" she said. "I don't want to live here anymore. I'm going to the Western Psychiatric Hospital right now! They can help me."

My mom and I said we didn't want her to leave. "We love you," we told her. But Shono called a taxi and left anyway.

While Shono was at the hospital, she fell twice and hit her head. After the second fall, she went into a coma. The staff at Western sent her to Presbyterian Hospital.

At this hospital Shono was put on a respirator. Then they took her off of it because she started breathing on her own. But she never came out of her coma. A couple of days later—the last day we visited her—she died. I watched her die.

I miss Shono every day. I loved her so much, and I know I always will. I never thought much about death before, but I think about it now. Sometimes I dream that Shono didn't die. I walk into our apartment and find her there. She's happy and well. But when I wake up, I know she's gone, and it's hard for me to keep from crying.

God bless our Shono. I pray He is taking good care of her. Every Sunday I light a candle for her at church.

Shono had a big stuffed toy—a brown mouse she called Basil. Before she left for the hospital that last time, she gave him to me. Basil used to sit on Shono's bed. Now he sits on mine.

Basil

A One-Parent Family

I never knew my father. He died before I was born. But I don't feel bad that mine is a one-parent family. I know a lot of kids whose fathers and mothers don't get along. They're always arguing and fighting. I wouldn't like that.

Some people believe a fatherless family doesn't have good children. Well, let me tell you something. Out of ten children in my family, nine have graduated from high school. Mom says any mother can and should see to it that her children finish high school. I don't plan to disappoint her. I'm determined to graduate from high school too.

Three of my sisters went to college. One graduated; one went three years before she quit; and the other one went two years. My brother Bob attended college for three years. My oldest brother Mickey was the first one in our family to graduate from college. He is now a newspaper editor.

If we didn't have to live here, I think we would have it all. My sisters are always trying to get my mother to move to Los Angeles. I wish we could move to California right now. My mom says no because she doesn't have the money to move and wouldn't have enough to live on once we got there. She refuses to be a burden to others. But I can't help but wish she would change her mind about going.

I would like nothing better than to wake up one morning and hear my mother say, "Anika, we are moving today!"

If I had my dream house, any child could skip rope on my sidewalk without being bothered by bullies or drunks.

Because many things have bothered me for so long, I have written my story about growing up in *The Ghetto*. It's not a very happy story, but I wrote how I felt. Now that it's down on paper, I feel better. I would like to think that someone, somewhere, will read my words.

If you have ever lived in a ghetto, you will understand what I have written. If you haven't lived in a ghetto, you'll never completely understand what I've said. But I can tell you this—you wouldn't like it there!

I know you would hate to live in a neighborhood of boarded up, empty houses and vacant lots where people dump trash everywhere. You would not like being surrounded by dope, alcohol, and loud and ignorant people who have loud and ignorant children.

I hope my mother and I will someday get out of our ghetto. I dream of having a nice, quiet place with a yard full of flowers. And I'd like to have both a front and a back porch.

I sometimes wish I could be like *Dorothy* in *The Wizard of Oz*. I wish a tornado would grab Mom and me up and blow us far away to another land.

But if that tornado never comes to take us away, or if I don't win the sweepstakes, or if no one helps us get out of here—then I will do it myself!

After I graduate from college, I am going to find a good job and I am going to get us out of here! Time has a way of passing fast, so it won't be such a long wait.

Someday we are going to have a nice house and plenty of food. And when Christmas comes, my mother isn't going to have to worry about having enough money to buy gifts. I will never forget the struggles my mother is going through. I know God is watching over us, and He will answer my prayers.

Someday!

I don't want to be someone else;
I just want to be myself.
I don't want to fly or have wings;
I just want the basic life things.
I dream of having enough money
    and owning a car,
Of lying safe on my porch
    and watching the stars.
I don't need a mansion—
    nothing like that, you see.
I just want a small house—
    a place with one or two trees.

I write this poem because it's the way I feel,
    and it's the way I am.

THE NATIONAL WRITTEN & ILLUSTRATED

— THE 1989 NATIONAL AWARD WINNING BOOKS —

Lauren Peters
age 7

Michael Cain
age 11

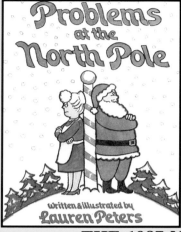

Problems at the North Pole
Written & illustrated by Lauren Peters

the Legend of SIR MIGUEL
written and illustrated by MICHAEL CAIN

WE ARE A THUNDERSTORM
written and photographed by amity gaige

—THE 1987 NATIONAL AWARD WINNING BOOKS—

Amity Gaige
age 16

JOSHUA DISOBEYS
Written and Illustrated by Dennis Vollmer

THE HALF & HALF DOG
written and illustrated by LISA GROSS

WHO OWNS THE SUN?
-written & illustrated by- STACY CHBOSKY

Dennis Vollmer
age 6

—THE 1989 GOLD AWARD WINNERS—

BROKEN ARROW BOY
WRITTEN AND ILLUSTRATED BY ADAM MOORE and his friends

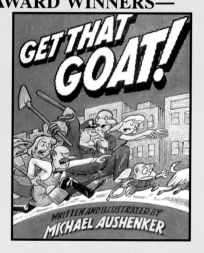

GET THAT GOAT!
WRITTEN AND ILLUSTRATED BY MICHAEL AUSHENKER

Lisa Gross
age 12

Students' Winning Books Motivate and Inspire

Each year it is Landmark's pleasure to publish the winning books of The National Written & Illustrated By... Awards Contest For Students. These are important books because they supply such positive motivation and inspiration for other talented students to write and illustrate books too!

Students of All Ages Love the Winning Books

Students of all ages enjoy reading these fascinating books created by our young author/illustrators. When students see the beautiful books, printed in full color and handsomely bound in hardback covers, they, too, will become excited about writing and illustrating books and eager to enter them in the Contest.

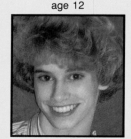

Stacy Chbosky
age 14

Adam Moore
age 9

Michael Aushenker
age 19

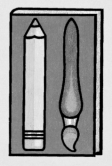

Enter Your Book In the Next Contest

If you are 6 to 19 years of age, you may enter the Contest too. Perhaps your book may be one of the next winners and you will become a published author and illustrator too.

BY... AWARDS CONTEST FOR STUDENTS

— THE 1988 NATIONAL AWARD WINNING BOOKS —

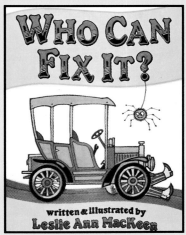

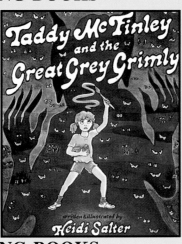

Leslie Ann MacKeen
age 9

—THE 1986 NATIONAL AWARD WINNING BOOKS—

Elizabeth Haidle
age 13

Heidi Salter
age 19

— THE 1985 GOLD AWARD WINNERS —

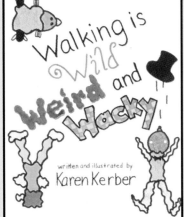

Amy Hagstrom
age 9

Isaac Whitlatch
age 11

Winners Receive Contracts, Royalties and Scholarships

The National Written & Illustrated by... Contest Is an Annual Event! There is no entry fee! The winners receive publishing contracts, royalties on the sale of their books, and all-expense-paid trips to our offices in Kansas City, Missouri, where professional editors and art directors assist them in preparing their final manuscripts and illustrations for publication.

Winning Students Receive Scholarships Too! The R.D. and Joan Dale Hubbard Foundation will award a total of $30,000 in scholarship certificates to the winners and the four runners-up in all three age categories. Each winner receives a $5,000 scholarship; those in Second Place are awarded a $2,000 scholarship; and those in Third, Fourth, and Fifth Places receive a $1,000 scholarship.

To obtain Contest Rules, send a self-addressed, stamped, business-size envelope to: THE NATIONAL WRITTEN & ILLUSTRATED BY... AWARDS CONTEST FOR STUDENTS, Landmark Editions, Inc., P.O. Box 4469, Kansas City, MO 64127.

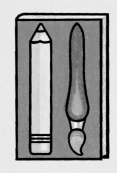

Karen Kerber
age 12

David McAdoo
age 14

Dav Pilkey
age 19

THE WRITTEN & ILLUSTRATED BY... CONTEST
— THE 1990 NATIONAL AWARD WINNING BOOKS —

Aruna Chandrasekhar
age 9

Anika Thomas
age 13

Cara Reichel
age 15

Jonathan Kahn
age 9

Jayna Miller
age 19

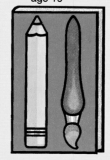

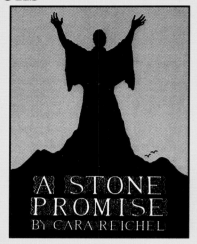

— THE 1990 GOLD AWARD WINNERS —

Winning the Gold Award and having my book published are two of the most exciting things that have ever happened to me! If you are a student between 6 and 19 years of age, and you like to write and draw, then create a book of your own and enter it in the Contest. Who knows? Maybe your book will be one of the next winners, and you will become a published author and illustrator too.

— Jayna Miller
Author and Illustrator
TOO MUCH TRICK OR TREAT